Original title:
When I Was Broken

Copyright © 2024 Swan Charm
All rights reserved.

Author: Kene Elistrand
ISBN HARDBACK: 978-9916-89-658-7
ISBN PAPERBACK: 978-9916-89-659-4
ISBN EBOOK: 978-9916-89-660-0

## Wholeness from the Worn

In the fabric of time, threads got frayed,
Worn edges tell stories, in shadows played.
Each tear a reminder, of battles fought,
In the heart's quiet corner, wisdom is caught.

Beneath heavy burdens, light softly seeps,
Through cracks in the armor, the spirit leaps.
A stitch brings connection, mends weary seams,
Finding strength in the cracks, we weave our dreams.

Rusty voices of ages, whispers untold,
Echo through valleys where beauty unfolds.
In the dance of the dusk, the twilight gleams,
Wholeness emerges from the fragments of dreams.

With every soft heartbeat, resilience grows,
In the soil of the past, a wildflower blows.
Petals in the wind, once torn, now renew,
Showing the world what a heart can do.

Embrace every mark, let the journey unfold,
For in flaws we find stories, in scars we are bold.
In a tapestry woven, our truths intertwine,
Wholeness from the worn, a beauty divine.

## A Tapestry of Resilience

Through storms we rise, we bend, we grow,
Threads of strength in our hearts do glow.
Each tear we shed, a stitch of grace,
Crafting stories, time will embrace.

With every fall, we stand once more,
A vibrant patchwork, rich in lore.
Fading scars, yet brightly shine,
A tapestry woven, forever divine.

## Echoes of Yesterday

In shadows cast, whispers remain,
Faint echoes of joy and pain.
Memories linger, soft and sweet,
Footsteps of time, never complete.

The past is a song, haunting yet true,
A canvas of dreams, painted blue.
Through every sigh, the heart will learn,
In history's fire, our spirits burn.

## Embracing the Splintered Self

In cracks and fragments, beauty lies,
A puzzle made of silent cries.
Each shard reflects a different hue,
A story whispered, ancient and new.

With arms wide open, we greet the pain,
A symphony played on life's refrain.
Through shattered dreams, the light may shine,
Embracing the pieces, all can align.

## Whispers from the Wound

From deep within, a silent plea,
Whispers float like leaves from the tree.
Wounds may bleed, still life will thrive,
Resilience blooms, the heart's alive.

Each hurt a lesson, softly taught,
In the stillness, battles fought.
With tender touch, we find our way,
Whispers of hope guide on the way.

## **Solace in the Shattered**

In pieces scattered wide and far,
Amidst the cracks, a subtle star.
Whispers of hope, a gentle touch,
In brokenness, we find so much.

Each shard a tale of love once bright,
Transforming shadows into light.
With every fragment, a new way found,
In the chaos, solace is profound.

## The Unraveling of Chains

Rusty links and echoes fade,
In the quiet, truths are laid.
Each step forward, a weight released,
In freedom's breath, the soul's increased.

The chains that held now turn to dust,
In this journey, we learn to trust.
Through trials faced, we rise anew,
In every scar, the strength shines through.

## Unseen Beauty in the Chaos

In swirling storms, a dance unfolds,
Amidst the chaos, stories told.
Colors clash and shadows blend,
In disarray, we find a friend.

Hidden gems, in grit they show,
From tangled roots, wildflowers grow.
In every tumult, grace remains,
Beauty thrives where chaos reigns.

## Silent Conversations with Loss

In stillness shared, a quiet grace,
Through whispered fears, we trace this space.
Each moment lingers, heavy yet light,
In absence felt, we find the right.

Memories pause, a gentle wave,
In every heart, the brave must brave.
Through silent talks, the soul will mend,
In loss's arms, we learn to bend.

## The Fragile Palette

Colors whisper on the edge,
Blending softly, warping truth.
Each stroke a tender promise,
A canvas of fragile youth.

Brushes dipped in sorrow's hue,
Leaving trails of dreams undone.
Yet the light breaks through the grey,
And the shadows start to run.

A palette rich with laughter,
Laughter dances in the air.
In the depths of every color,
There lies beauty beyond compare.

Spectrum weaves a story bright,
Painted with the pains we face.
Yet every flawed creation,
Wraps our scars in warm embrace.

So let the brush move freely,
Let every droplet find its way.
For in the fragile palette,
Life's true colors gently sway.

## Healing through the Cracks

In the pavement, life finds light,
Weeds push through with all their might.
Each fracture tells a story deep,
Of resilience where old wounds seep.

Through the gaps, a bloom will rise,
Filling spaces with bright surprise.
Nature whispers that we heal,
In the shattered, love reveals.

Cracked walls hold the tales of time,
Echoes of a heart that climbs.
In every break, a chance to grow,
Finding beauty in what we sow.

Let the sun warm all the scars,
Bathe the cracks in healing stars.
For every fracture, life transcends,
And through the pain, the heart mends.

So let the storms and shadows play,
For in the cracks, we find our way.
Healing whispers through the night,
In darkness, turns the wrong to right.

## Serenade of the Undone

Melodies weave through the haze,
A symphony of hopeful days.
In the quiet, voices call,
Echoing through each rise and fall.

Strings are plucked with gentle hands,
Winds carry songs across the lands.
In every note, a tale unfolds,
Of moments lost and mysteries told.

Rhythms dance like fleeting dreams,
In the dark, the heart redeems.
With every pause, a breath of fate,
Life's undone serenade, innate.

Harmonics find their solace sweet,
In the spaces where shadows meet.
Fragile whispers, bold and deep,
Awakening the soul from sleep.

So sing the serenade of time,
In every silence, find the rhyme.
For in the undone lies the truth,
A melody of lost sweet youth.

## Transitions of Tenderness

The dawn melts into the day,
Softly wild in its array.
Tender hues of gold collide,
In transitions where dreams reside.

Leaves dance lightly in the breeze,
Whispers echo through the trees.
Every shift, a story shared,
Through the passage, hearts are bared.

Moments shift like gentle tides,
Emotions rise, where love abides.
In the flow from night to light,
Tenderness guides us to what's right.

Closing eyes on shadows cast,
Finding peace in the contrast.
For every season, soul takes flight,
In transitions held tight, so bright.

So let the world shift and sway,
In tenderness, we find our way.
Through each change, we learn to trust,
That love's embrace is always just.

## **The Beauty in Imperfection**

In cracks where light finds grace,
A story etched in time and space,
The flaws, they dance with quiet pride,
In every scar, a truth to guide.

The crooked path, a tale to tell,
Of journeys passed, we know so well,
A tapestry of broken threads,
In life's embrace, perfection sheds.

A chipped vase holds water's glow,
In uneven lines, the heart can flow,
Rough edges soften with the years,
They cradle all our hopes and fears.

Embrace the shadows, let them blend,
Imperfection is a loyal friend,
In every stumble, beauty grows,
A masterpiece in all that shows.

## **Journeys Beyond the Fall**

Through valleys deep, the rivers wind,
Across the hills, the air is kind,
Each step we take, a lesson learned,
In every fall, new strength is earned.

The mountains stand, both bold and grand,
A reminder of a guiding hand,
We stumble forth, resolve to rise,
Finding hope in the vast skies.

With every bruise, there's beauty found,
In whispered winds, our dreams abound,
A path unknown, we walk with grace,
For every fall, there's a new place.

The light may fade, but stars ignite,
Leading us through the endless night,
In journeys vast, our spirits soar,
Embracing life, forevermore.

## Sifting Through the Shards

Amidst the glass, reflections gleam,
Fragments whisper, come and dream,
In chaos found, a heart can mend,
Through shattered pieces, hope ascends.

With careful hands, we gather light,
Creating beauty from the blight,
Each jagged edge a story speaks,
In the silence, strength it seeks.

The shards may cut, but wisdom grows,
In every pain, the spirit knows,
To pick apart the past with care,
In healing, we find love to share.

From scattered dreams, new visions weave,
In the fragments, we believe,
To hold the broken, we must start,
In every shard, beats a bold heart.

# The Dawn of Restoration

In stillness wakes the morning sun,
A gentle light, the day's begun,
With every dawn, we start anew,
In hope's embrace, we find our view.

The past may haunt, like shadows cast,
Yet time reveals, it cannot last,
With every breath, release the weight,
For life awaits, let's celebrate.

In tender moments, hearts align,
Through broken paths, old dreams entwine,
The dawn restores what's lost and torn,
In whispered grace, a spirit born.

We lift our eyes to skies so wide,
In the horizon, hope abides,
The journey's long, but joy ignites,
In dawn's embrace, we reach new heights.

## **From Ashes to Embers**

In the stillness of night,
Dreams whisper low and bright.
From the darkness, we rise,
Softly lit by fireflies.

Hope flickers in the air,
In the glow, spirits dare.
We rebuild from the past,
Embers warm, shadows cast.

In the heart of despair,
There's a spark everywhere.
With each step, we ignite,
Turning shadows to light.

Together we will soar,
With courage, we explore.
From ashes, new dreams bloom,
In the brightening room.

The journey's never done,
With embered hearts, we run.
Through the dusk and the dawn,
We will carry on strong.

## The Tenderness of Cuts

In the silence of night,
Shadows dance in the light.
Each scar tells a story,
Of pain wrapped in glory.

Beneath the skin so thin,
Lie battles lost and wins.
What breaks us makes us whole,
Tenderness in the soul.

The blades we wear with pride,
Healing hearts open wide.
For every fractured piece,
There's a whisper of peace.

Love lingers like a song,
In the places we're strong.
Tiny cuts shape our skin,
But love is where we begin.

Through the tears we will find,
The beauty intertwined.
In the tenderest cuts,
Life's lessons are what it puts.

## **Unraveled Threads**

In the fabric of time,
Each moment, a soft rhyme.
Threads woven, colors blend,
Stories tied without end.

As patterns fall away,
New shapes begin to play.
From chaos, beauty flows,
In the dance of the folds.

With every stitch we mend,
We find a way to bend.
Unraveled, we are free,
To discover what we see.

Life's loom, a gentle hand,
We craft what we have planned.
In threads both thick and thin,
We weave the light within.

The tapestry unfolds,
In colors bright and bold.
In each unraveling strand,
There's a new life at hand.

## **New Beginnings**

In the dawn's tender glow,
An awakening flow.
A fresh page to ignite,
Everything feels so bright.

Throw the shadows away,
Embrace a brand new day.
With a heart open wide,
Let the journey decide.

Each step holds a chance,
In the rhythm, we dance.
With hope leading the way,
We'll find what we can say.

Look to the sky so clear,
Feel the magic near.
In the whispers of time,
Life's blessings, a sweet rhyme.

New beginnings await,
As we open the gate.
Together, hand in hand,
In the light, we will stand.

## Journeying Through my Cascade

Winding paths that we roam,
Each step leads us back home.
In the flow of the stream,
Life unveils a grand dream.

With the whispers of leaves,
Nature gently believes.
Every moment we share,
Is a breath filled with care.

Through the rush and the calm,
Find the heart's soothing balm.
Amidst the splashes and spray,
We discover our way.

Each cascade tells a tale,
Of the storms we prevail.
Let the waters inspire,
As we climb ever higher.

In this journey we trace,
Find the joy, find the grace.
Through the ups and the downs,
Wear our laughter like crowns.

## **Beneath the Surface of Despair**

In shadows deep where secrets lie,
A weight unseen, the heart's dry sigh,
Each breath a struggle, whispers frail,
Beneath the tides, the hopes grow pale.

The moonlight flickers, dimmed by cries,
A lonely echo, fading ties,
Yet through the fog, a flicker glows,
A spark that fights, though silence grows.

The rivers churn with hidden fears,
Yet strength resides within the tears,
Each droplet tells a tale of woe,
Yet speaks of paths that dare to show.

The weight of sorrow bends the soul,
But hope can stitch what pain stole whole,
Through murky waters, light may pierce,
And beauty hides where hearts disperse.

So rise, dear heart, from depths so dark,
The dawn will break with a gentle spark,
For though the night may hold you vast,
The dawn's embrace will free at last.

## **Unraveling in Silence**

Alone within the quiet space,
Thoughts drift like clouds in an endless race,
Words unsaid stir like autumn leaves,
In whispered tones, the heart deceives.

Each tick of time, a memory fades,
In shadows cast, the spirit wades,
Beneath the stillness, storms collide,
Yet longing blooms where fears reside.

A fragile thread binds hopes and dreams,
Yet silence reigns, or so it seems,
In breaking dawn, the truth will rise,
As hidden songs break through the lies.

The echoes linger, softly call,
In silence deep where shadows sprawl,
Yet through the tear, a voice will break,
To weave the threads that silence takes.

From quiet depths, a strength will swell,
To find the light, to break the spell,
And in the void, a heart will bide,
For silence holds what words can't hide.

## The Strength of a Thousand Shards

In fragments scattered, beauty lies,
Each shard reflecting countless skies,
Though broken pieces tell of pain,
They shimmer bright in darkest rain.

A heart once whole, now weathered stone,
Yet in each crack, a spark is sown,
The strength that rises from the fall,
Each piece a story, every call.

Beneath the weight of all that's lost,
The spirit learns to bear the cost,
From shattered glass, a prism glows,
In every cut, the courage grows.

Embrace the wounds, let laughter swell,
For in each mark, a tale to tell,
The strength of shards, a fire ignites,
A dance of colors on cold nights.

So gather up the pieces near,
And mend the heart with love, not fear,
For in the cracks, the light will find,
The strength of shards, beautifully intertwined.

## **Traces of a Once Whole Self**

In echoes faint of days gone by,
A whisper soft, a gentle sigh,
Traces linger on the soul's skin,
Of moments lost and where we've been.

In fragments left of who we were,
A ghostly dance, a distant blur,
Yet in each step, a truth remains,
A melody that softly reigns.

The heart remembers what's been lost,
Each path we took, each bridge we crossed,
In silent rooms where shadows play,
The self once whole now fades away.

Yet in the ruins, seeds are sown,
And from the past, a strength is grown,
For every thread that falls apart,
Can weave anew within the heart.

So cherish traces, learn to see,
The beauty in what used to be,
For in the loss, we find the gain,
And from the ashes, rise again.

# The Weight of Splintered Soul

In shadows cast by time's embrace,
A fractured heart finds no safe place.
Each shard reflects a hollow truth,
Echoes of a forgotten youth.

Beneath the surface, silence cries,
A whisper caught in tranquil lies.
With every breath, the burden grows,
The weight of pain that no one knows.

Broken dreams and faded light,
Haunted by the endless night.
But still the soul longs to be free,
To heal the wounds and find the key.

The shards, they glisten, sharp and bright,
Yet hold a beauty in their plight.
A tapestry of lost desires,
That flickers softly, never tires.

So let the pieces fall away,
And forge anew a brighter day.
From splintered souls, a strength can rise,
A phoenix born from whispered sighs.

## **Scars Tell Stories**

Each scar upon this weary skin,
A tale of battles lost and won.
They speak of courage, fear, and grace,
Of every struggle we must face.

In lines and marks, the past remains,
A map of joy intertwined with pains.
Each wound a lesson, each cut a fight,
A testament to courage in the night.

From fiery trials, we emerge anew,
In every scar, a strength to pursue.
They whisper secrets of survival,
Of grace through grief, of fierce revival.

A story written on fragile flesh,
A canvas marked by every press.
Embrace the scars, let them shine bright,
For in their presence, we find our light.

So wear them proud, these etched respects,
For every scar, a bond connects.
They tell of hope and fights well-fought,
In every story, the lessons taught.

## Out of the Ashes

From embers cold, a spark ignites,
A flicker born from darkest nights.
In silent breaths, the ashes wake,
A promise tied to what we stake.

The flames of sorrow slowly pass,
Yet in their wake, we find our glass.
From shattered dreams, new visions bloom,
A garden grown from autumn's gloom.

With every tear, a river flows,
Resilience found where hardship grows.
Through tangled branches, light breaks through,
A testament to all we knew.

The phoenix rises, strong and bold,
Defying fate, a soul consoled.
In flight, it bears no weight of fear,
For life renews with every tear.

Out of the ashes, life takes flight,
In scars and wounds, we find our light.
A journey forged in fire's embrace,
Emerging whole, we claim our place.

## A Symphony of Loss

Each note we play, a heartbeat's sigh,
The echoes of a sweet goodbye.
In every chord, a memory sways,
A symphony of love through days.

With strings that quiver in the night,
We dance with shadows, wrapped in light.
In silence held, our spirits soar,
A melody we can't ignore.

The rhythm pulses, heartbeats clash,
In every tear, a haunting crash.
The beauty found in what we miss,
A song composed of love's sweet bliss.

Through loss, we learn to find the grace,
In every silence, we find our place.
The whispers of joy through sorrow's song,
A harmony that pulls us along.

So let the music softly play,
A symphony that guides our way.
In every note, a love survives,
Forever echoing, our hearts alive.

**Tides of the Heart**

Whispers roll in soft caress,
Moonlight dances on the sea.
Each wave brings a sweet address,
Yearning love set wild and free.

In the night, our shadows play,
Echoes sweet within the breeze.
We drift and sway, come what may,
Hearts entwined like ancient trees.

Tides that pull and tides that push,
Gently shaping every shore.
In their rhythm, thoughts can rush,
Endless longing, evermore.

When dawn breaks, colors ignite,
Casting dreams on sands of gold.
In the warmth of morning light,
All our stories yet untold.

So let the ocean be our guide,
Through the storms and tranquil days.
With each ebb, we'll turn the tide,
Together walking love's vast ways.

## **Into the Fray of Healing**

Step by step through shadows cast,
Braving storms that block the sun.
With each breath, the die is cast,
Healing battles fought and won.

Every scar a chapter penned,
In the book of me and night.
Ways to break and then to mend,
Seeking solace in the light.

Voices soft, they call my name,
Hope ignites in whispered prayer.
In the chaos, I reclaim,
Every piece that's lying bare.

Journey winding, filled with fright,
Yet I walk this path with grace.
Filled with dreams to take flight,
Finding strength in every place.

So I rise, unbound, awake,
With each dawn, the world will clear.
Into the fray, I will stake,
My own truth, I hold it dear.

# **Fragments of a Forgotten Self**

Once I danced in hues of gold,
Lost in laughter, light, and bliss.
Now I wander, tales untold,
Seeking echoes in the mist.

Whispers haunt the empty air,
Memories like shadows creep.
Versions of me, unaware,
Surface dreams that dare to leap.

In the silence, fragments rise,
Pieces glinting in the dark.
Revealing truths beneath the lies,
Fires once dimmed now leave a spark.

Tattered hopes and crumpled plans,
Yet from rubble, beauty grows.
With open heart, I take my stand,
Reclaimed spirit softly glows.

So I gather my lost parts,
Weaving stories, bold and bright.
With each stitch, I heal my heart,
Into the gleam of new-found light.

## **Labyrinth of Lost Pieces**

Lost within a winding maze,
Searching for the way back home.
In the shadows, thoughts ablaze,
Through these halls of fear I roam.

Each corner holds a whispered past,
Echoes of a life once known.
Questions linger, shadows cast,
In the dark, I'm not alone.

Tangled threads of fate and dreams,
Guide me through the winding path.
In the silence, hope redeems,
Finding joy within the wrath.

With each turn, a lesson learned,
Fragments of the self arise.
In the struggle, strength is earned,
Courage blooms as passion dies.

So I'll tread the maze with grace,
For the journey shapes my soul.
In each step, the promise placed,
That I, too, can be made whole.

## **Unveiling the Broken**

In shadows deep, the silence reigns,
A heart once whole, now wears the chains.
Fragments whisper in the dark,
Dreams long lost, they leave a mark.

Each tear a story, softly told,
In brittle hands, we grasp the cold.
Yet in the cracks, a spark remains,
Hope blooms gently, despite the pains.

Through every wound, a lesson learned,
From ashes rise the fires burned.
We mend the seams with threads of grace,
In brokenness, we find our place.

The world will see, our scars like art,
A tapestry of a healing heart.
Together we'll unveil the true,
The beauty found when we break through.

## **The Light Beneath the Surface**

Beneath the waves, a shimmer glows,
Secrets lie where no one knows.
In oceans deep, the silence hums,
The tale of light is what it sums.

Ripples dance on the water's face,
Whispers echo of hidden grace.
The darkness fades as dawn will break,
With every wave, the shadows shake.

Bright hues clash in the watery realm,
Nature's art takes over the helm.
Each moment filled with life anew,
A dance of colors, a vibrant hue.

From depths we rise, the journey starts,
With every beat, we mend our parts.
The heart unfolds like petals wide,
As light emerges, so shall pride.

## In the Wake of Fractures

In quiet moments, echoes dwell,
Stories form, like magic spells.
Shattered dreams upon the floor,
Yet from the shards, we'll build once more.

Fractures tell of battles fought,
In whispered tones, the lessons taught.
Through every scar, a glimpse of grace,
In the wake of pain, we find our place.

When shadows rise and fears entwine,
We'll seek the light, let hope align.
For every fall, there's strength to gain,
In the brokenness, we break the chain.

The heart that mends is not the same,
Awakening the spirit's flame.
In the wake, new dreams will spark,
A future bright, ignited from dark.

## Reclamation of the Heart

A heart once lost in silent cries,
Wandering through the endless skies.
But time will heal the aching void,
Through love and kindness, pain destroyed.

With gentle hands, we reclaim the past,
Building bridges that long will last.
Each heartbeat sings a vibrant tune,
Dancing beneath the silver moon.

The strength resides in every thread,
The tapestry of life we've led.
In pieces scattered, hope takes flight,
Restoring balance, shining bright.

Together we rise, stronger, whole,
A journey shared, it fills the soul.
The reclamation is a sacred art,
A beautiful tale of the healing heart.

## **The Strength of Shattered Pieces**

In the dark of broken dreams,
A glimmer fights to shine,
Each shard holds a whisper,
Of hope, so divine.

From fragments, we gather,
Our spirit takes flight,
In the depths of our sorrow,
We unearth the light.

Embracing the mess,
We mend what we lost,
With courage in hand,
We count every cost.

Through tears and through trials,
We forge our own fate,
In the strength of our pieces,
We find love, we create.

So, let the shards shimmer,
In the canvas of night,
For in their reflection,
We manifest might.

## Beyond the Veil of Suffering

Beyond the heavy curtain,
Where silence holds sway,
A whisper calls softly,
To chase shadows away.

In pain there's a lesson,
A seed deeply sown,
Through darkness we wander,
Yet we're never alone.

Each scar tells a story,
Of battles we've fought,
A testament woven,
In the lessons we've sought.

Through heartache and longing,
We rise from the fall,
With wings made of courage,
We answer the call.

Beyond suffering's veil,
There's beauty to find,
In the journey of healing,
Our souls intertwined.

## **Navigating Through Turbulence**

In the storm's fierce embrace,
We stand side by side,
With sails made of whispers,
And hearts open wide.

The waves may come crashing,
Yet we hold our ground,
Through shadows and turmoil,
Our strength knows no bound.

Each gust a reminder,
To stay true and bold,
In the dance of the uncertainties,
We learn to be gold.

With stars as our compass,
We chart out the night,
In the chaos of change,
We ignite the light.

So let the winds howl,
And the tempests arise,
For in navigating turbulence,
We discover our skies.

## Carrying the Weight of Strain

Beneath the heavy burden,
We take one more stride,
Through valleys of worry,
We walk with pride.

With shoulders that tremble,
And spirits so weary,
We find strength within,
Though the path seems dreary.

Each step that we take,
Is a mark of our grace,
In the weight of our trials,
We find our own place.

For every heavy load,
There's resilience to gain,
As we learn to lift others,
In the midst of our pain.

So carry the burden,
With love and refrain,
For in sharing the journey,
We lessen the strain.

## **Breaths Amidst the Shattered**

In the silence where echoes dwell,
Fragments whisper tales to tell.
Shattered dreams upon the floor,
Yet with every breath, we soar.

Amidst the ruins, hope ignites,
Glimmers bright in darkest nights.
Life's pulse beats in fractured ways,
With each breath, the spirit sways.

In the tension of lost and found,
Resilience rises, so profound.
Though the world may seem in shards,
Strength grows fierce, disregards.

Every crack holds light anew,
Wounds that heal and weave the true.
From the depths, a new song swells,
In the shattered, love compels.

Together we mend what's torn,
In our hearts, a fire, reborn.
With breaths shared, we shall dance,
Amid the shards, we take our chance.

# **Echoes of the Fractured**

Crisp are the sounds of silence here,
Echoes linger, sharp and clear.
In the cracks where shadows play,
Fractured dreams begin to sway.

A melody of loss and gain,
Resonates through joy and pain.
Whispers come from broken walls,
In stillness, every heartbeat calls.

Ripples of hope in the despair,
Life unfolds, a breathless prayer.
In tones of sorrow sweetly sung,
From fractured chords, we are sprung.

Washed in echoes of the past,
Lessons learned, and shadows cast.
In the fractures, light can seep,
Through every wound, our spirits leap.

We gather echoes, heal the cracks,
Embrace the splintered, no turning backs.
Together we rise, unconfined,
In fractured notes, our hearts aligned.

## **Yearning for Wholeness**

In the spaces between the cracks,
Yearnings weave through silent tracks.
Fingers reach for what is lost,
Craving warmth, despite the frost.

Whispers dance on fragile wings,
Calling forth what memory brings.
In the vastness where shadows play,
Hope emerges, lighting the way.

An ache for unity we feel,
In every wound, a chance to heal.
Through the fragments, hearts entwine,
Seeking solace, love divine.

With every step, we draw the near,
Each heartbeat echoes what we fear.
Yet in the yearning, strength is found,
Through shattered pieces, we rebound.

Yearning binds us, soul to soul,
In the struggle, we become whole.
Together we rise, firm and strong,
In every fracture, we belong.

## Celestial Cracks in the Flesh

Stars embedded deep in skin,
Celestial light, where dreams begin.
Cracks reveal the cosmic dance,
In shadows, bright souls take a chance.

Galaxies swirl within our veins,
Each heartbeat sings of joy and pains.
Through the rifts, we find our place,
In celestial bonds, we embrace.

Wounds remind us of the fight,
And within darkness, we find light.
Cracks in flesh, a sacred space,
For the universe's tender grace.

From every scratch, a story blooms,
In every scar, a future looms.
Celestial echoes brush the scars,
Reminding us we're made of stars.

As we walk through this earthly quest,
In cracked celestial, we find rest.
Pulling love from all we've known,
Through our fractures, we have grown.

# Frost Upon the Heartstrings

In winter's grasp, emotions freeze,
Silent echoes in the trees.
Crystalline dreams begin to fade,
Love's warmth wrapped in a cold cascade.

Beneath the snow, the heart beats slow,
A flame tucked deep, yet still aglow.
Each icy breath, a tale of old,
A story whispered, yet untold.

Through frozen paths we walk alone,
Searching for a love, our own.
With every step, the frost may bite,
But hope still glimmers in the night.

When spring arrives and thaw unfolds,
Soft petals bloom from rime so bold.
The heartstrings thaw, and music plays,
Awakening dreams through sunny rays.

In every flake, a memory found,
A love's embrace, a gentle sound.
For even frost cannot restrain,
The warmth that blossoms after rain.

## **From Abyss to Ascent**

In shadows deep where fears reside,
A heart can quake, a soul can hide.
But through the void, a whisper's call,
A flicker shines, a hope for all.

With every doubt, a step to climb,
Embracing pain, we weather time.
From depths of dark, the light will break,
Transforming scars that make us wake.

Upward we soar, the skies expand,
With every trial, we take a stand.
Resilience builds with each new breath,
Defying shadows, conquering death.

The spiraled path may twist and turn,
Yet in our hearts, there burns a yearn.
To rise beyond what holds us back,
To find the strength we often lack.

So from the abyss, we take our flight,
Chasing dreams with all our might.
Each rising sun, a brand new start,
From darkest depths, we grace the heart.

## Shards of Resilience

In broken pieces, beauty lies,
Reflections dance in tear-filled eyes.
Each shard a tale, a path once crossed,
Of battles fought and love that's lost.

Yet from the fragments, strength can grow,
A tapestry of pain and glow.
With gentle hands, we stitch anew,
Mending spaces, crafting true.

The colors merge in vibrant hue,
A canvas born from all we knew.
In every crack, a light can seep,
A promise made to never sleep.

Each scar, a marker of the fight,
A testament to inner light.
Through trials faced and lessons learned,
A fire ignites, the heart's discerned.

So let the world see what we've made,
A brilliant soul, unafraid.
For in each shard and fractured dream,
Lies resilience, a radiant beam.

**Fractured Whispers**

In quiet corners, secrets hide,
Fractured whispers, love's divide.
Each word a puzzle, a fractured song,
In silent hearts where hopes belong.

The echoes linger, soft and sweet,
A memory laced in bittersweet.
With every sigh, an untold pain,
A longing dance that leaves a stain.

Through fractured paths, we weave our fate,
In every glance, love's heavy weight.
Yet through the cracks, the light still breaks,
Awakens dreams that fear forsakes.

So let the whispers guide the way,
For in the night, comes dawn's array.
With hope as our compass, we'll ignite,
The fractured whispers into light.

And as we mend what's torn apart,
A symphony ignites the heart.
From every fracture, strength is born,
In whispers soft, we meet the morn.

**Pieces Untold**

Fragments scattered on the floor,
Memories whisper, tales of yore.
Silent echoes in the night,
A puzzle waiting for the light.

Hearts that ache, stories unseen,
Behind closed doors, we dream and glean.
Every shard a life once whole,
Stories woven into the soul.

Time will gather what was lost,
In the silence, we pay the cost.
Restoring grace to what was frail,
Finding strength within the pale.

Secrets held in tender hands,
We forge a path across the sands.
Every piece a step we take,
In the shadows, hope won't break.

Together we will find our way,
Through the night, into the day.
Healing starts with every fold,
In the heart, our pieces told.

## Resilience in Ruins

Amidst the ashes, new life grows,
A testament to strength that shows.
From broken paths, we rise anew,
In each disaster, a clearer view.

Nature whispers with a gentle sigh,
Roots entwined reach for the sky.
In every crack, resilience thrives,
We find the will, we learn to strive.

Structures crumble, yet we stand,
Rebuilding dreams with steadfast hand.
From the ruins, we seek the bright,
In the darkness, we find our light.

Hope like ivy climbs the walls,
In every fall, a voice that calls.
Strengthened by the storms we've faced,
With every scar, our lives are laced.

Resilience shines where shadows dwell,
In every heart, a silent swell.
Though the past may leave us bruised,
In the struggle, we are infused.

## **Cracks of Light**

In the darkness, a flicker gleams,
Through the cracks, we chase our dreams.
A subtle glow in endless night,
Reminders that we'll be all right.

Each fracture tells a tale of hope,
In the brokenness, we learn to cope.
Beneath the weight, a heart beats true,
In the quiet, a promise grew.

Light will seep through weary seams,
Illuminating faded themes.
Every crevice holds a chance,
Inviting us to join the dance.

Finding beauty in the flawed,
A tapestry of paths well-trod.
From every shadow, colors blend,
In the light, our fears suspend.

Together we will brave the dark,
Guided by that tiny spark.
In the cracks, new journeys start,
Weave the light into the heart.

## Mending the Tapestry

Threads of life entwined and torn,
In the weavings, we are worn.
Every stitch a story told,
In the fabric, warmth unfolds.

Colors fade but love remains,
In the mending, joy sustains.
With gentle hands, we sew the seams,
Binding dreams with delicate beams.

Worn and frayed, yet rich with grace,
In the shadows, we find our place.
Every loop a memory shared,
In the tapestry, hearts have bared.

With each patch, a healing sound,
Life's imperfections all around.
Together, we create anew,
In the mending, we find our crew.

Mending time with threads of care,
In the tapestry, we lay bare.
A vibrant whole from parts we weave,
In this journey, we believe.

# The Transformation of Pain

In shadows deep where sorrows lie,
The heart beats slow, a heavy sigh.
From ashes rise, a flicker bright,
The dawn breaks through the endless night.

With every wound, a lesson learned,
Through fiery trials, the spirit burned.
A tapestry of scars unfolds,
In pain, a tale of courage told.

The chains of grief begin to fray,
As hope emerges, lighting the way.
Resilience grows from whispered cries,
Embracing strength as weakness dies.

Transformed by storms that shaped the soul,
From shattered pieces, we feel whole.
In every tear, a spark of grace,
The journey of our sacred space.

So let the pain be not in vain,
For through the dark, we find our gain.
In transformation's gentle hand,
We rise anew, together stand.

## **Colors of a Scarred Soul**

A palette bright of every hue,
Reflecting battles fought and true.
Each scar a mark of stories spun,
In colors bold, the life we've won.

Crimson shades of deep despair,
Shadows whispering in the air.
Yet through the gloom, the gold peeks through,
With each new dawn, a chance to renew.

Blues of sorrow, the tears we've shed,
Greens of growth where hope has bled.
Violets soft, the love we share,
A rainbow formed from pain laid bare.

The brushstrokes of our journey blend,
In vivid tales that never end.
From every shade, a brighter whole,
The canvas speaks of a scarred soul.

Embrace the colors, let them be,
A testament to you and me.
In every scar, a beauty glows,
In life's vast art, the spirit grows.

## Shattered But Not Shy

Fragments scattered, lost apart,
Yet still beats a hopeful heart.
In every crack, a story speaks,
Resilience strong, though the spirit peaks.

With courage drawn from broken places,
I stand unmoved, defying graces.
Each shard reflects a strength unseen,
A light that shines where dark has been.

Though shattered glass can cut so deep,
It holds the promise that I keep.
In boldness found, I rise each day,
More than the sum of pieces lay.

Embracing flaws, I find my worth,
In imperfect truths, I claim my birth.
No longer shy to show my scars,
I wear them bright like shining stars.

In battles fought, I'm bruised but brave,
From shattered dreams, a spirit saves.
I will not hide, I won't retreat,
For strength is found in love, complete.

## Rebirth from Ruin

In silence deep, the ground lays still,
From ashes rise a stronger will.
With every end, begins the flow,
A seed of hope begins to grow.

Through mighty storms, the roots intake,
From broken ground, new life awake.
What once was lost now takes its form,
In the heart of chaos, we transform.

Tears like rain will nurture ground,
In every whisper, life is found.
From darkness blooms the brightest light,
In shadows deep, we take our flight.

With every wreckage, chance to build,
A spirit fierce, a heart fulfilled.
In ruins lies the chance to grow,
Rebirth from pain, a vibrant show.

So take the ashes, craft anew,
For in the struggle, strength ensues.
With open arms, embrace the dawn,
From ruin, rise—an endless song.

# Harmony from Dissonance

In the chaos, a chord is found,
Birds sing sweetly, all around.
The storm whispers, softly tamed,
From shadows, a new song is claimed.

Voices blend, no longer torn,
The night gives way to a new dawn.
Hearts unite, differences fade,
In this embrace, love is made.

Each note lifts, like a gentle breeze,
Bringing peace, as time does tease.
Strangers dance, hand in hand,
In this place, together we stand.

Minds open, to ideas unfurled,
Building bridges, across the world.
From discord, a symphony rise,
Played in harmony, beneath the skies.

Through the struggle, beauty grows,
In the rhythm, the spirit flows.
With every breath, we find our way,
Harmony reigns, come what may.

# The Phoenix of the Heart

From ashes, a spark ignites,
In darkened skies, it takes flight.
A flame within, ever bright,
Rising again, out of the night.

Wounds heal slowly, but they mend,
Strength emerges, curves and bends.
The heart knows how to reclaim,
Loss transforms, it's not the same.

Through trials faced, the spirit learns,
And in the fire, passion burns.
Courage found in bitter times,
New life stirs, like vibrant chimes.

With wings spread wide, the soul ascends,
In every tear, the hope extends.
Beauty crafted from each scar,
The fire of love, our guiding star.

Yearning deep, a new path drawn,
A symphony swells, rebirth at dawn.
Through the struggle, we ignite,
The phoenix rises, into the light.

# **Ripples of Healing**

In still waters, a pebble tossed,
Echoes of hope, never lost.
Each ripple whispers, soft and true,
The heart's journey, anew we pursue.

Kindness spreads, like the morning dew,
Nurturing souls, in shades of blue.
Touching lives, with gentle hands,
Together we rise, love understands.

Moments shared, a bond that grows,
Through laughter, healing light flows.
Like rivers that bend, we find our way,
In the warmth of friendship, we choose to stay.

Stories woven, through time and space,
A tapestry bright, each thread finds its place.
In every heart, a spark resides,
Ripples of healing, where love abides.

Together we rise, through every quest,
In unity forged, we find our best.
The water's dance, a sacred art,
From ripples of love, we never part.

## The Veil of Restoration

Behind the veil, the shadows weave,
A tapestry of what we believe.
Restoration whispers in the night,
Guiding lost souls back to light.

In quiet corners, hope resides,
Patiently waiting, as time slides.
Every tear, a seed is sown,
From broken ground, new life has grown.

Veils of sorrow, lifted high,
Revealing truths, as stars collide.
Courage found in the gentle sway,
Restoration beckons, come what may.

The dance of time, a rhythmic flow,
Embracing the past, as we grow.
Each heart story, a bridge to mend,
Together we rise, our spirits blend.

Through layers soft, the light shines through,
A promise kept, in all we do.
With every dawn, a chance restored,
In the weave of life, love is adored.

# The Strength in Weakness

In shadows deep, we find our way,
A quiet strength that holds the sway.
With trembling hands, we rise and stand,
Embracing flaws, we make our stand.

Through whispered doubt, our spirits soar,
In every crack, we'll seek for more.
The heart, though worn, still shines so bright,
It's in the pain, we find our light.

Resilience blooms in fields of grief,
A tender hope, our sweet relief.
In weakness lies a hidden grace,
A journey shaped, we face with pace.

Though storms may bend and break our will,
Our roots run deep, we stand still.
In every fall, we learn to rise,
Our spirit fierce, we claim the skies.

So when you doubt what you can face,
Remember strength finds its own place.
In every tear, a lesson learned,
The fire within, forever burned.

## Glue of Forgotten Memories

In dusty corners, stories lay,
Fragments of life in soft decay.
A whisper here, a laugh over there,
The glue of memories fills the air.

Time weaves through both joy and pain,
An endless thread that does remain.
Moments lost but not erased,
In fading light, they're still embraced.

We gather pieces, hearts collide,
In every smile, the past resides.
Holding tight, we feel the pull,
Of love that swells and moments full.

With every glance, the echoes ring,
Of laughter shared and hearts that sing.
For in the cracks, our stories bloom,
The scents of life, the sweet perfume.

So cherish all that's been and gone,
In every note, a timeless song.
The glue of memories, strong and true,
Will bind our hearts through all we do.

## Cracks in the Canvas

Beneath the paint, the truth is bare,
In every flaw, a tale to share.
The canvas tells of battles fought,
In every crack, a lesson sought.

Brush strokes wild, yet beautiful still,
A vibrant blend of strength and will.
Each fracture holds a whispered rhyme,
A testament to space and time.

Life's portrait drawn in shades of grey,
Yet through the cracks, the light finds way.
The broken parts, they tell a tale,
Of storms endured and hearts that sail.

So let the colors bleed and fade,
In every scar, a beauty made.
Embrace the flaws that speak so loud,
For in the cracks, we stand so proud.

Our lives, a work of art divine,
Each blemish part of the design.
In imperfections, life's dance begins,
Through cracks, our hearts, they beat and spin.

## Weaving Light from Darkness

In shadows deep, the weaver stands,
With threads of gold, in tender hands.
From darkest nights, a vision grows,
With every stitch, a story flows.

The loom of life, both strong and frail,
Each fiber tells of hope's soft trail.
Through silent fears, we find our way,
Creating light from shades of gray.

The fabric woven, rich and vast,
With dreams and whispers of the past.
In every hue, a lesson glows,
A tapestry of joy and throes.

So when the night seems hard to bear,
Remember light is woven there.
With every thread, a path is laid,
In darkness, brighter hopes are made.

Together weaving, hand in hand,
We turn the night to brighter land.
For every shadow holds a chance,
To weave the light, our souls advance.

## Shadows of Yesterday's Pain

Whispers haunt the silent night,
Memories wrapped in fading light.
Echoes of laughter, now just a sigh,
Shadows dance as we pass by.

In the corners of weary hearts,
Each scar tells where the healing starts.
Time moves on, but feelings stay,
Carried forth in today's gray.

Ghosts of choices, lost in the fade,
Lessons learned, and dues paid.
Through the darkness, hope can gleam,
Mending the seams of a fractured dream.

Yet in the shadow, strength is born,
A light emerges from the scorn.
Courage found in each refrain,
Transforming whispers of yesterday's pain.

So we rise, with scars in tow,
Embracing the past, we continue to grow.
In every step, a flicker remains,
Illuminating shadows of yesterday's pains.

## **From Splinters to Strength**

Amidst the shards of broken trust,
Lies the power that we must.
Fractured dreams, like scattered glass,
Yet we rise, as shadows pass.

With every cut, wisdom unfolds,
Stories of courage yet to be told.
From the pain, resilience springs,
Healing whispers, the heart still sings.

Splinters deep, but spirits soar,
Through the trials, we seek more.
Each bruise a badge, each tear a song,
A symphony of where we belong.

Stripped bare, yet fiercely whole,
Strength is forged within the soul.
From the ashes of all we've lost,
We bloom anew, no matter the cost.

The journey shapes us, just like clay,
From splinters forged, we find our way.
Embracing scars, embracing strife,
Building a path to a stronger life.

## **Footsteps on Broken Glass**

Every step a fragile sound,
Echoes shatter on the ground.
With each crack, a story told,
Footprints marked in shards of gold.

Navigating paths of jagged years,
Carrying the weight of whispered fears.
Yet in the pain, we find a song,
Melodies of righting the wrong.

The heart may ache, the spirit bend,
But through the hurt, we shall transcend.
Finding beauty in the strife,
In the glass, the dance of life.

Resilience written on our skin,
Each mark a testament within.
On shattered dreams, we gently tread,
From broken glass, new hopes are bred.

So we walk with courage clear,
Finding strength in every tear.
Through the fragments, we will pass,
Creating paths on broken glass.

## **Navigating the Cracked Path**

With careful steps, we tread the way,
Each crack a choice in the light of day.
Beneath our feet, the ground may shake,
But we venture forth for courage's sake.

Whispers of doubt may fill the air,
Yet hope's bright spark remains our glare.
As we navigate the fractured lane,
In each stumble, growth will reign.

The road is long, the journey wears,
Yet every burden, the heart shares.
Finding strength in the cracks we find,
Woven threads of the heart and mind.

Through the shadows, a guide appears,
Illuminating paths through our fears.
In this maze, the truth will show,
That light can break through even the low.

So onward we move, hand in hand,
Together we rise, together we stand.
Navigating life's wild, cracked path,
Finding joy where once was wrath.

## **Whispers of the Wounded**

In shadows deep, they softly sigh,
Broken dreams beneath the sky.
With weary hearts, they search for light,
In silent battles, lost from sight.

They bear the scars, a tale untold,
Of hopes once bright that turned to cold.
Yet in the pain, a strength does bloom,
From shattered souls, new roses loom.

Whispers echo in the night,
Of lives reborn, of inner fight.
With every tear, resilience grows,
In fractured paths, true beauty shows.

They rise from depths, the weary soul,
Embracing fate, they feel the whole.
For in their wounds, a story's weaved,
Of battles fought and dreams retrieved.

## **The Beauty in Splinters**

In broken wood, there lies a grace,
Each jagged edge, a tender space.
With colors warm and textures rough,
In every flaw, we find enough.

Splintered pieces tell of time,
Of strength that grows through every climb.
For nature's art, in chaos found,
Manifests beauty, all around.

Shattered glass reflects the sun,
A myriad of hues that run.
In every crack, a story's spun,
Of what was lost, and yet, the fun.

From remnants worn, new dreams arise,
In whispered tales beneath the skies.
In splinters bold, we dare to see,
The hidden charm of mystery.

## **Rebuilding from Ashes**

In the stillness after flames,
Life emerges, unbroken names.
From soot and smoke, a spark ignites,
In darkest hours, new hope unites.

With courage strong, they rise anew,
Each heart a promise, pure and true.
From ashes cold, they span the skies,
With wings of fire, they learn to fly.

Brick by brick, they pave the way,
Creating paths where they can stay.
In the rubble, a vision grows,
Of brighter days and healing flows.

From scorched remains, a garden's born,
With fragrant blooms and daylight's crown.
In every scar, a tale designed,
Of strength and grace in heart entwined.

## A Journey Through the Cracks

Through tiny gaps, the light breaks in,
A journey starts where shadows spin.
With cautious steps, they tread the lines,
In every crack, new hope defines.

The whispers call from deep below,
In crevices, the wildflowers grow.
With vibrant hues against the gray,
They teach the heart to find its way.

Each stumble feels like falling down,
Yet in each fall, they find the crown.
For life's a dance of rise and fall,
In broken paths, they hear the call.

Through jagged edges, love takes flight,
In every tear, a spark of light.
They journey on, with spirits bold,
In every crack, a story's told.

## Portrait of a Weary Heart

In shadows deep, the heart does sigh,
With weary beats that never fly.
Each longing glance, a silent plea,
A portrait framed, yet never free.

Eyes like clouds, burdened with rain,
Carrying the weight of hidden pain.
In every smile, a story lies,
A weary heart that slowly cries.

Memories linger, haunting yet bright,
Chasing hopes that fade with night.
In every echo, a soft farewell,
A heart unchecked in its own hell.

Time's gentle touch can soothe or cut,
Yet still we stand, as if we're shut.
A canvas stained with shades of gray,
Portraying love that slipped away.

Yet in the dusk, a flicker glows,
A promise whispered, though it slows.
For even weary hearts must start,
To rise again, and mend their art.

# **When Dreams Turned to Dust**

Once, dreams danced beneath the stars,
Filling our minds with hopes from afar.
But time, it stole the spark and flame,
Leaving us with emptiness and shame.

Promises whispered in twilight's breath,
Now echo softly like whispers of death.
Caught in a web of faded plans,
Where laughter dwindles and silence spans.

Grains of hope slip through our hands,
As we stand on forgotten lands.
Each vision blurred, each wish undone,
What once was bright now hides from the sun.

In empty rooms where memories fade,
Shadows of dreams, unmade and frayed.
Still, we brace against the dusk,
Hoping to find what we no longer trust.

Yet in the dust, a seed may lie,
Waiting for rain and a fresh blue sky.
When dreams turn to dust, we must believe,
In the power of hope, we can still achieve.

## **Beneath the Surface of Pain**

Beneath the waves of sorrow's tide,
Where sorrow's whispers often hide.
Lies a world where silence reaps,
And shadows linger, then the heart weeps.

In quiet corners, the secrets dwell,
Crafted echoes of a broken bell.
Untold stories weave through the night,
Beneath the surface, out of sight.

Every bruise a gentle mark,
Stories etched within the dark.
Like stars obscured by clouds that loom,
Our pain rests softly, breeding gloom.

Yet in this depth, resilience swells,
Emerging from forgotten wells.
For every tear that softly falls,
Breaks the chains and gently calls.

Beneath the surface where shadows lay,
Truth glimmers like a dawning day.
In every wound, a lesson gained,
Beneath the surface, we are unchained.

# Dreaming in the Fractured Light

In fractured light, the world is skewed,
A fragile heart finds solace brewed.
Shadows dance where hopes collide,
Yet dreams persist, refusing to hide.

With each small crack, new paths are drawn,
Flickers of dawn on a weary lawn.
We tread through corners, lost yet found,
In the whispers of a quiet sound.

Stars scatter like thoughts in flight,
Painting the canvas of the night.
Each glimmer tells of battles fought,
In the fractured light, we seek what's sought.

Though fears may rise like tides at sea,
We still dare to dream, to simply be.
In the broken shards, our truths take form,
An ember glowing through the storm.

Dreaming in light that bends and breaks,
We gather strength for our own sakes.
For in the cracks, we find the grace,
To turn our silence into space.

## A Mosaic of Pain

Shattered dreams lie on the ground,
Pieces scattered all around.
Each fragment tells a tale so deep,
Of silent cries and sleepless sleep.

A canvas painted in hues of gray,
Faded memories that linger and stay.
Lines etched deep in weary faces,
A reminder of lost embraces.

Through the cracks the light will seep,
In the void where echoes creep.
Beauty found in every scar,
A mosaic of who we are.

Yet twilight whispers softly near,
Holding close what we fear.
In the darkness, stars may gleam,
A flicker of hope, a distant dream.

From the ashes, we shall rise,
With wisdom gleaned from weary sighs.
In the pieces, we find our song,
Embracing where we all belong.

## The Language of Scar Tissue

Words unspoken, wounds that bind,
Carved in silence, lost in time.
A language known by those who bleed,
In every cut, there lies a seed.

The whispers of a heart laid bare,
In shadows past, the weight we bear.
Stories etched in every line,
A testament of pain divine.

Memories linger, ghosts that haunt,
In the quiet, our souls confront.
Each scar a chapter, bold and true,
The language of life, a vivid hue.

Through the darkness, strength we find,
A symphony of heart and mind.
In the echoes of our strife,
We weave together the fabric of life.

Healing starts with tender grace,
In the embrace of time and space.
From the ashes, we start anew,
Speaking the truth that's carved in blue.

## Dancing with Fragments

In the twilight where shadows fall,
Fractured dreams begin to call.
A waltz of pieces, lost yet found,
Every turn, a sorrowed sound.

Each misstep a story shared,
In the dance of hearts laid bare.
With every twist, the past reveals,
An echo of what once was real.

To the rhythm of broken grace,
We twirl in our sacred space.
The fragments shimmer, a beauty rare,
Dancing in the depths of despair.

In the movement, hope ignites,
We find our way through endless nights.
In the chaos, we learn to sway,
Finding strength in our own ballet.

So let us dance, though it may ache,
With every step, new paths we'll take.
In the fragments, we unite,
A dance of souls in shared twilight.

## **Beneath the Weight of Sorrow**

A heavy heart, an endless night,
Beneath the weight, we seek the light.
In silence spreads a fearsome depth,
Each breath a chain that binds with theft.

Yet in the dark, a whisper plays,
A glimmer through the heavy haze.
We carry burdens, worn and steep,
Yet in those shadows, hope can creep.

The tears that fall like gentle rain,
We gather all the ache and pain.
With every droplet, strength will swell,
In the depths, we learn to dwell.

A heart that's broken learns to mend,
Through sorrow's touch, we make our friend.
With time, the burdens turn to wings,
And in the struggle, wisdom sings.

For beneath the weight, we're not alone,
In the silence, our hearts have grown.
Together we face the coming dawn,
Beneath the weight, our hope lives on.

## **Healing in the Shadows**

In the silence, whispers flow,
Gentle breezes start to blow.
Stars above begin to gleam,
As we weave a fragile dream.

Wounds will heal in muted light,
Hiding pain, a quiet fight.
With each breath, we find our way,
Through the night into the day.

Leaves that fall, they dance on air,
In the quiet, learn to care.
Each step forward, brave and true,
Finding strength in shades of blue.

Time will mend the fractured heart,
Piece by piece, we'll make a start.
Trust the journey, trust the call,
From the shadows, we stand tall.

In the end, we'll rise anew,
Shining bright, a different hue.
From the darkness, light will stream,
Healing found within the dream.

# The Melodies of a Crumbled Dream

In the echoes of the night,
Faded tunes take gentle flight.
Whispers haunt the quiet space,
Carrying a lost embrace.

Once bright colors, now a blur,
Memories, they start to stir.
In the heart, a longing song,
As we search where we belong.

From the ashes, notes arise,
Wishful hopes and silent sighs.
Fragments dance upon the breeze,
Painting dreams among the trees.

In the twilight, shadows play,
Melodies that drift away.
Yet within each broken chord,
Lies a tale to be restored.

So let the music softly flow,
In the aftermath, we grow.
Though crumbled, hope remains alive,
In the songs that help us thrive.

## Ghosts of a Broken Past

In the corners, shadows creep,
Whispers of the secrets keep.
Ghosts that linger, tales to tell,
Of moments lived and farewells.

Echoes dance on empty floors,
Memories knock on forgotten doors.
Haunting weaves a bitter thread,
Of paths once walked, now left for dead.

As the sun begins to rise,
Light will pierce the darkened skies.
With each dawn, a chance to heal,
Finding truths we can reveal.

Through the loss, we find our way,
In the scars, the strength will stay.
From the ruins, flowers bloom,
Turning darkness into room.

So let the past be guide, not chain,
In the heart, release the pain.
Ghosts may fade but wisdom stays,
Lighting up our future ways.

## **Threads of Hope**

Woven tightly, dreams entwined,
In the tapestry, hope defined.
Each new strand, a whisper heard,
In the silence, hearts prefer.

With every pull, a story weaves,
Through the pain, the heart believes.
Colors bright against the gray,
Threads of hope will guide the way.

In the fabric of each hour,
Glimmers light, an inner power.
Wounds may fray but love will tie,
A united bond, we'll fly.

Hope's embrace, a gentle hand,
In the storm, we take our stand.
Together, we can make it through,
Knowing well, our dreams renew.

So hold on tight, and do not fear,
Each thread spun with love is near.
Through the struggles, we will cope,
In the darkness, threads of hope.

## **Splintered Dreams**

In the quiet night, shadows creep,
Fragments of hope, buried deep.
Whispers of wishes, lost in the air,
Yearning for futures, layered with care.

Pages are turning, stories untold,
Flickering visions, daring and bold.
Each splintered path, a tale of its own,
Mending the pieces, through seeds we've sown.

Stars dance above, guiding the way,
Through jagged edges, night turns to day.
Dreams take flight, like birds set free,
Embracing the unknown, just wait and see.

A heart in pieces, yet beats so strong,
Finding new rhythms, where we belong.
With every heartbeat, we rise once more,
Splintered, yet soaring, always explore.

From shattered visions, we weave our fate,
In the cracks of sorrow, we cultivate.
Illuminated paths, through scars we tread,
In splintered dreams, new beginnings spread.

## **The Light After Dusk**

When the sun bows down, stars ignite,
A world transformed, cloaked in night.
With every twilight, shadows descend,
The promise of dawn, around the bend.

Soft whispers echo, the night unfolds,
Stories of wonder, patiently told.
In the quiet moments, solace is found,
A dance of silence, where dreams abound.

The moon's gentle gaze, a calming balm,
In darkness, we find a healing calm.
Embracing the stillness, hearts set free,
We bloom in the shadows, like the ancient trees.

Hope flickers bright, like candles aglow,
Guiding us forward, with a soft glow.
Each star a wish, each breath a prayer,
In the light after dusk, we learn to dare.

As dawn approaches, colors ignite,
Transforming the darkness, birthing the light.
With every sunrise, the promise is clear,
The light after dusk, dispelling our fear.

**Discovering Wholeness in Fragments**

In broken pieces, we hide our hearts,
Searching for solace, where healing starts.
Each jagged edge tells stories of past,
In fragments, we learn that love can last.

Puzzle of moments, scattered and wild,
Every shard a memory, cherished and filed.
Through the cracks, we find strength anew,
In every disaster, resilience grew.

Embracing the gaps, we gather each part,
Building a mosaic, a work of art.
From chaos to order, we shape what's true,
Discovering wholeness in what we pursue.

In the depths of struggle, a light will beam,
Illuminating pathways, weaving our dream.
With every setback, we rise from despair,
Finding our unity in love and care.

From fragments to fullness, the journey unfolds,
Creating a tapestry, rich and bold.
In discovering wholeness, we learn and mend,
Embracing our stories, with each heart we send.

# A Canvas of Resilience

On life's canvas, colors collide,
Brushstrokes of heartache, beauty, and pride.
Every splatter of pain, a tale engraved,
With shades of our struggles, our spirits are saved.

In the face of storms, we find our voice,
Painting with passion, we rise by choice.
Each mark tells a story, of battles we've fought,
In each hue, a lesson, wisdom once sought.

Layered with courage, we persevere,
Creating our masterpiece, year after year.
In the frame of existence, we find our way,
A vibrant reminder of brighter days.

Through shadows and light, we sketch our truth,
Reveling in moments, embracing our youth.
In every iteration, our spirit shines bright,
A canvas of resilience, ignited by light.

As new colors blend, we evolve and grow,
In the art of becoming, our essence will show.
With each stroke of courage, we break every chain,
On this canvas of life, beauty will reign.

## The Echo of Fragments

In the stillness, whispers play,
Reflections of what slipped away.
Memories dance on fragile air,
Each moment lost, a silent prayer.

Shards of laughter, echoes faint,
Brush of sorrow, hues of paint.
Carved in time, the heart does ache,
Yet beauty blooms from every break.

Through broken dreams, we find our way,
Guided by light of yesterday.
A tapestry of life unfolds,
With stories deep and truths retold.

Silhouettes of what we were,
In every breath, a gentle stir.
Fragments weave a world anew,
In every piece, a spark shines through.

Witness the echoes, soft and clear,
Carrying whispers, close and near.
In each fragment, a heart beats strong,
Together they sing, a timeless song.

## A Mosaic of Lost Dreams

Across the canvas, colors blend,
Pieces scattered, yet transcend.
Shattered hopes in patterns weave,
A story told by those who grieve.

In golden hues, the past reflects,
A fractured heart in its defects.
Each fragment holds a tale untold,
A picture rich, a life of gold.

With every shard, we stitch and mend,
Creating paths where sorrows end.
In brokenness, we learn to see,
The beauty in our history.

Lost aspirations, like fallen leaves,
Gathered up by life's gentle eaves.
In rust and dust, the hope remains,
A mosaic formed from both joys and pains.

Through the chaos, order grows,
In the ruins, new life flows.
Together we stand, strong and free,
In a world shaped by destiny.

# Rebuilding the Unseen

Amidst the rubble, dreams arise,
Brick by brick, we touch the skies.
Hands together, hearts aligned,
In the shadows, strength we find.

With every dawn, we start anew,
Crafting futures bright and true.
Unseen realms, they start to gleam,
In the silence, we find our dream.

The scars we bear tell tales of fight,
In the darkness, we seek the light.
Through storms we've weathered, paths we've crossed,
From every gain, we learn the cost.

Resilience blooms in hardened soil,
From every tear, a new that's loyal.
In the unseen, hope takes flight,
Beneath the rubble, shines the bright.

With courage, we rise from the ash,
Building bridges where once was crash.
Rebuilding souls, we'll never cease,
In unity, we find our peace.

## **Illuminating Shadows**

In twilight's glow, shadows dance,
With flickering lights, they take a chance.
In the darkness, secrets swirl,
Illuminated, the truth will unfurl.

Every corner, a story told,
In chiaroscuro, we find the bold.
Soft whispers echo through the night,
Guiding dreams toward the light.

The night reveals what day conceals,
In hidden spaces, the soul heals.
Through shadows deep, we learn to see,
The layers of possibility.

Together we walk this winding path,
Embracing both joy and the aftermath.
With every step, we cast our glow,
Illuminating the tales below.

So let the shadows play their role,
As we journey deep within our soul.
In the interplay of dark and light,
We find our truth, pure and bright.

## **Growth Amidst the Fractures**

In cracked soil, a sprout emerges,
Winds of change will guide its way.
Sunshine breaks through darkened urges,
Hope unfolds with each new day.

Roots reach deep, embracing struggle,
While fragile leaves will stretch and sway.
From broken ground, loud dreams will smuggle,
Life finds light in earth's ballet.

Petals dance in morning's dew,
Whispers of resilience rise.
Nature's strength will see it through,
In the shadows, beauty lies.

Each crack tells a story true,
Of battles fought, and lessons learned.
In every scar, there's strength to pursue,
From ashes, new fires are burned.

So fear not the shattering quake,
For in breaks, life finds its path.
From fractures, fresh dreams will awake,
Growth will blossom from the wrath.

## The Dance of Lost Moments

Memories float like autumn leaves,
Whirling softly, a fleeting waltz.
We hold tightly to what deceives,
Chasing echoes, counting faults.

Every glance a whisper's sigh,
Time slips by like grains of sand.
In the silence, dreams will cry,
Longing for a tender hand.

Footsteps fade in fading light,
The shadows cast our yesterdays.
In dreams, we find our hearts take flight,
Embracing both the lost and haze.

The pulse of life beats slow and fast,
In every heartbeat, sweetness stings.
We dance to echoes of the past,
Where every moment lightly clings.

Though time may steal our cherished days,
In memories, we bend and sway.
Lost moments weave in soft displays,
A dance of past in present's play.

## Secrets of the Unbound

In wild woods where silence sprawls,
Whispers linger on the breeze.
Nature's heart through starlit calls,
Secrets whispered, hidden keys.

Roots entwined in night's embrace,
Quiet truths beneath the skin.
In shadows deep, an ancient trace,
Unseen worlds call out within.

The ocean's song reveals its lore,
Waves that crest with tales untold.
In the depths, the spirits soar,
Through lost realms, both young and old.

Mountains guard the sky's pure light,
Crags that cradle dreams and fears.
In their majesty, what a sight!
Each horizon shedding tears.

Secrets held in nature's hand,
Stories woven in the air.
In the unbound, we will stand,
Finding solace everywhere.

## **Redemption in Redemption**

In the dusk of weary days,
We seek light in shadows cast.
Hope ignites in gentle rays,
From shattered pasts, our souls are massed.

Fingers trace the scars we've made,
With each touch, a story flows.
In every wound, a strength conveyed,
Redemption blooms where sorrow grows.

Forgive the echoes that remain,
Letting go of burdens, free.
For in the loss, we find our gain,
A dance of peace, a new decree.

Rise from ashes, fierce and bold,
Let the heart's fire warm the night.
In every tale of heartache told,
Redemption's door will shine so bright.

Through trials faced and bridges crossed,
We learn to love what once was pain.
In every journey, never lost,
Redemption's touch, our souls regain.

## The Art of Healing

In the quiet dawn, hope gently stirs,
Whispers of comfort, like soft mild purrs.
Each tender moment, a step to the light,
Breathe in the warmth, let go of the night.

Time drips slowly, like honey on bread,
With every heartbeat, new threads can be spread.
Pain's heavy burden, a shadow to cast,
Yet in this journey, I'm learning at last.

Colors return, where once shades of gray,
Transforming the scars into art on display.
A canvas of stories, both jagged and bright,
Reminders of battles fought, won in the night.

Joy sprouts like flowers in fields once so bare,
Each petal a promise, a whisper, a dare.
To embrace the healing that softly draws near,
Finding the strength in the love that is here.

So I walk this path, with a heart that is whole,
Mending the edges, reclaiming my soul.
In every heartbeat, a rhythm of grace,
The art of healing, my sacred embrace.

## Mending in Silence

In shadows where whispers of solace reside,
Mending in silence, where secrets confide.
The quiet embraces, the stillness of heart,
Here in the hush, we make a new start.

Threads woven gently through fabric of night,
Stitched with the stars, they shimmer and light.
Each pull of the needle, a promise to keep,
Together we gather, through silence profound and deep.

Voices unspoken, yet heard in the mind,
Every soft silence, a bond that we find.
The distance we cover in moments unseen,
Mending in silence, where love can convene.

With hands that are tender, we weave and we mend,
A tapestry forged where starting meets end.
No need for the echo of clamor and noise,
In the silence we thrive, in the stillness, rejoice.

So let us remain in the calm of our hearts,
Finding our peace, where the mending imparts.
In the quiet we grow, in the hush we ignite,
Mending in silence, two souls taking flight.

## **Pieces of a Shattered Heart**

Broken shards glimmer under the light,
Fragments of love scattered, lost to the night.
Each piece a memory, a moment once shared,
A reminder of passions that kindled, then flared.

Collecting the remnants, I search through the maze,
Revisiting whispers, and warm summer days.
With every reflection, the pain finds its voice,
Yet in the heart's rubble, I dare to rejoice.

Colors collide in the chaos amassed,
A mosaic of lessons from heartache amassed.
From sorrow arises resilience anew,
In pieces of pain, my spirit breaks through.

I gather the fragments, assemble my truth,
With courage ignited, reclaiming my youth.
Each shard holds a story, no longer apart,
Together they dance in my mending heart.

So watch as I rise from the ashes once more,
With pieces united, I'm ready to soar.
From shattered to whole, I'll paint my own art,
Creating a masterpiece—my brave, fresh heart.

**From Ruins, I Rise**

Amidst the wreckage, a spark ignites,
Echoes of courage that banish the frights.
From ruins I gather the dust of my past,
Each moment a lesson, a shadow to cast.

The ashes of heartache, they shape and define,
A phoenix is born where the embers align.
With wings made from sorrows, I soar to the skies,
From the depths of despair, a new spirit flies.

Hope whispers softly, a song in the wind,
Each note a reminder that strength lies within.
Through trials and turmoil, I find my own way,
From the ruins of yesterday, I seize the new day.

Fires may scorch, but they also create,
A fertile ground where resilience will sate.
From the rubble, I rise, determined and bold,
My journey a tapestry, vibrant and gold.

So here I stand tall, grounded yet free,
A testament forged from what once used to be.
From ruins to triumph, my spirit defies,
In the heart of destruction, look—there I rise.

## Shattered Reflections

In mirrors cracked, truths take flight,
Whispered shadows steal the light.
Dreams once bold, now faintly glow,
Fragments fall where silence flows.

The past reflects in shards so clear,
Each piece a memory we hold dear.
Crimson hues of time untold,
In every crack, a story unfolds.

A heart once full, now feels the strain,
In every fracture, a hint of pain.
Yet in the darkness, hope ignites,
A tapestry of endless nights.

We gather pieces, one by one,
Beneath the weight of life's cruel sun.
Healing starts with gentle grace,
A dance of time in a sacred space.

Though shattered, light begins to weave,
In every cut, a chance to believe.
Reflections mend, embrace the scar,
In shattered glass, we find who we are.

# Fragments of a Lost Soul

In the silence, echoes call,
Whispers of a heart that stalls.
Shattered dreams on a dusty floor,
A soul adrift, forevermore.

Pieces scattered, lost in time,
Searching for a reason, a rhyme.
Each fragment holds a story frail,
In the essence of a silent wail.

Desires worn, like tattered cloth,
In shadows deep, I wander, lost.
Yet within this void of gloom,
A spark ignites, dispelling doom.

The journey's long, but I must tread,
Through paths of grief where angels led.
In every tear, a lesson sprouted,
In every sorrow, hope rerouted.

Amongst the wreckage, light breaks through,
A soul reborn, a heart anew.
Fragments join, mosaic bright,
The beauty made from endless night.

Through shadows thick, I will prevail,
In fractured pieces, love's sweet tale.
A lost soul finds its way back home,
In every step, no more to roam.

# Echoes of a Fractured Heart

In twilight's glow, the echoes sound,
A heart once whole, now is unbound.
Memories linger, soft and sweet,
In every beat, the past we meet.

A gentle tear, a whispered sigh,
Every note a reason why.
Through shadows cast, the light will rise,
In brokenness, new dreams arise.

For every echo in the night,
Brings forth the dawn, a fresh delight.
Fractured still, yet strong and bold,
In every story, love retold.

The scars we bear, the wounds they bear,
Tell of battles fought with care.
Yet through the pain, a rhythm flows,
In echoes soft, the heart still glows.

Transformation blooms from fear's embrace,
In fractured chords, we find our grace.
The symphony of scars will sing,
In every crack, a thriving spring.

So let the echoes softly play,
A fractured heart will find its way.
In love's embrace, we'll mend the sound,
In every echo, joy is found.

## The Art of Healing Scars

With tender hands, we shape our fate,
In every wound, a chance to create.
The art of healing, a painter's brush,
On canvas raw, we find our hush.

In every scar, a story lives,
The pain once sharp, now softly gives.
We weave our tales with threads of gold,
In healing's light, we're free and bold.

Colors blend, both dark and bright,
In healing strokes, we find the light.
The past remains, but now we grow,
In every scar, our strength will show.

The art of scars, a dance divine,
Through every hurt, the stars align.
With each brushstroke, we learn to soar,
In every flaw, forevermore.

So here's to wounds that once did ache,
In healing's grace, we find the break.
A masterpiece, our lives will be,
In every scar, a tapestry.

The art we craft through joy and pain,
In life's rich canvas, love will reign.
With every scar, a journey's mark,
The art of healing ignites the spark.

**Moments of Resurgence**

In twilight's glow, new dreams arise,
From ashes cold, under darkened skies.
Whispers of hope, soft winds comply,
Ingentle hearts, courage will fly.

Quiet reflections, embers ignite,
Starlit paths, embrace the night.
In every scar, a story lives,
Resilience grows, and heart forgives.

With every dawn, a fresh embrace,
Awakening strength, in life's swift race.
In fleeting moments, beauty unveils,
Through fleeting trials, our spirit sails.

Beneath the weight, we choose to stand,
Gathering hope with open hands.
Each tear that falls brings life anew,
In the quiet, strength imbues.

So let us rise, as phoenixes do,
With wings outstretched, kiss skies of blue.
In moments fleeting, we find our way,
To forge the light of a brand new day.

## **Breathing Life into Ruins**

Amid the rubble, flowers bloom,
Resilient beauty pierces gloom.
Nature's promise, in cracked stone,
Whispers sweetly, we're not alone.

The past may haunt with shadows long,
Yet in decay, we find our song.
The heart beats loud in desolate places,
Crafting joy in familiar faces.

With every gust, the wind will change,
Old scars will fade, new paths arrange.
Life finds ways in silence deep,
In abandoned spaces, dreams will leap.

From ancient walls, bright colors soar,
Stories of hope, forevermore.
In fragments scattered, we create,
A canvas rich with life's estate.

Let eyes discover the art in pain,
From every loss, there's much to gain.
In the ruins, life takes flight,
Breathing warmth into the night.

## The Embrace of Imperfection

Cracks in the vase hold tales untold,
Flaws give character, hearts grow bold.
In the chaos, beauty's found,
In every stumble, love is crowned.

The art of life, a patchwork quilt,
Stitched with dreams and hopes we've built.
Each jagged edge, a gentle grace,
Imperfections reflect our embrace.

Beneath the surface, colors blend,
Hearts as one, on which we depend.
The world a canvas, vast and wide,
In the flaws, we take great pride.

Moments slip; we learn to forgive,
In this dance, we choose to live.
Every heartbeat, a joyful song,
Embracing all that feels so wrong.

So let us cherish each little crack,
An ode to life, in its melodic track.
For in this journey, love remains,
The beauty found in life's refrains.

## **Finding Grace in the Breaks**

In the fractures, light seeps in,
Through shattered moments, we begin.
Grace unfurls in spaces wide,
When hope's soft whisper is our guide.

The heart learns well from weight of stone,
In silent battles, we are not alone.
Each break a lesson, bright and deft,
In every ending, something left.

We wear our scars like armor true,
Each one a story, each one a clue.
With open hands, we cradle fate,
Finding strength in the heart's debate.

Where dreams collide, paths intertwine,
Through tangled roots, we learn to climb.
Life's ebb and flow, a graceful dance,
In fleeting moments, we take a chance.

So, let us tread through trails of strife,
In every break, discover life.
With grace as compass, love our song,
Together, much can right the wrong.

## **Maps of a Shattered Heart**

Lines of pain drawn on old maps,
Each tear a landmark, each ache a trap.
In the wind's whisper, I hear your name,
Fragmented dreams caught in the flame.

Paths once shared now distant roads,
Carrying the weight of unspoken codes.
Memories scattered like dust in the air,
Tracing the contours of love laid bare.

Stars that once shone fade into the night,
Guiding lost souls, searching for light.
Every heartbeat a pulse in the dark,
Mapping the silence, igniting a spark.

With ink of sorrow, I sketch my fears,
Drawn with the quill of forgotten years.
Each stroke a whisper, each line a plea,
In this shattered heart, I long to be free.

## In the Wake of Collapse

Rubble scattered across the ground,
Echoes of laughter no longer found.
Buildings that stood like giants proud,
Now mere shadows beneath the cloud.

Each corner turned reveals the cost,
Of dreams once held, now all but lost.
Whispers of hope beneath the dust,
Truth twisted in the maze of mistrust.

Shattered glass reflecting the sun,
A fractured world where all is undone.
Yet in the chaos, a glimmer appears,
In the wake of sorrow, resilience cheers.

Silent spectators watching the fall,
Wounds in the heart, weary spirits call.
Through the ruins, a path is drawn,
A promise of life with each new dawn.

## **Regrowth from Defeat**

Beneath the ashes, seeds of hope lie,
Nurtured by tears that have dared to cry.
In the shadows of loss, strength takes root,
From the soil of scars, blossoms salute.

Each struggle a lesson, each wound a guide,
To rise anew, with courage and pride.
The heart learns to dance in the face of despair,
A vibrant rebirth ignites the air.

With hands outstretched, the past is released,
Embracing the present, the soul finds peace.
Growth is a journey, not just a race,
Fuelled by the fire of love's warm embrace.

And when the storms have finally passed,
Fertile ground blossoms, memories cast.
In every setback, we gather the light,
Regrowth from defeat, a powerful sight.

## **Lessons in the Lattice**


Threads of life woven, intricate and fine,
Patterns emerging, by design divine.
Each twist a story, each turn a fate,
In the tapestry of time, we contemplate.

Whispers of wisdom in knots that bind,
Teaching the heart to be gentle and kind.
In every challenge, a chance to grow,
Lessons in the lattice, strength in the flow.

Colors blend together, vibrant and bold,
In the loom of existence, new tales unfold.
Each layer a journey, each stitch a time,
Building connections, creating the rhyme.

With patience and care, we mend the seams,
In the woven patterns, we find our dreams.
Together we build, through joy and strife,
Lessons in the lattice, the fabric of life.

Milton Keynes UK
Ingram Content Group UK Ltd.
UKHW022225251124
451566UK00006B/126

9 789916 896